# What Would Jesus Do?

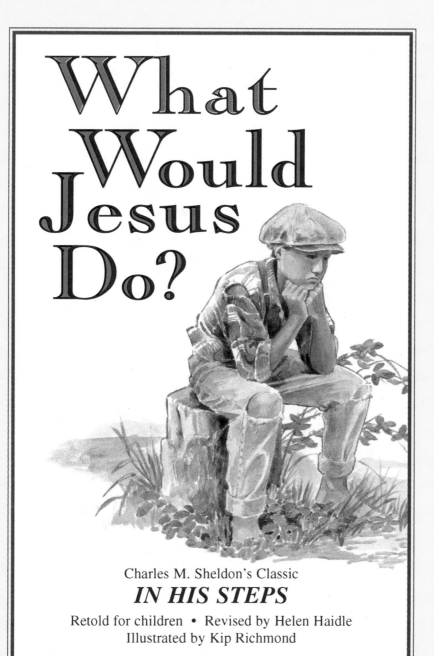

Charles M. Sheldon's Classic
### *IN HIS STEPS*
Retold for children • Revised by Helen Haidle
Illustrated by Kip Richmond

**Zonderkidz**
*The Children's Group of ZondervanPublishingHouse*

# TABLE OF CONTENTS

Chapter One      Picnic Stranger      5

Chapter Two      The Problem      13

Chapter Three      Hard Questions      19

Chapter Four      Taking Time      25

Chapter Five      New Friends      33

Chapter Six      High Hopes      39

Chapter Seven      Big Decisions      45

Chapter Eight      Stormy Night      51

Chapter Nine      A Lost Jump Rope      57

Chapter Ten      Coal Valley Neighbors      65

Chapter Eleven      A Reminder      73

Chapter Twelve      Claire's Decision      80

Chapter Thirteen      Claire's Fear      87

Chapter Fourteen      Finding Treasure      92

Chapter Fifteen      The Greatest Treasure      99

Chapter Sixteen      Trouble Time      106

Chapter Seventeen      The Warning      113

Chapter Eighteen      A Chance to Tell      119

Chapter Nineteen            Coal Valley Surprise    125
Chapter Twenty              Facing the Fire!        132
Chapter Twenty-One          Fighting the Fire       139
Chapter Twenty-Two          After the Fire          147
Chapter Twenty-Three        Fall Carnival           154
Chapter Twenty-Four         Big Award!              160
Chapter Twenty-Five         Train Trip              166
Chapter Twenty-Six          Ticket Trouble          171
Chapter Twenty-Seven        Cousin Amy              177
Chapter Twenty-Eight        Moving Troubles         185
Chapter Twenty-Nine         A Big Mistake!          191
Chapter Thirty              Lost and Alone          197
Chapter Thirty-One          Another New Friend      205
Chapter Thirty-Two          Big Bullies             211
Chapter Thirty-Three        In Jail                 217
Chapter Thirty-Four         Big Plans               223
Chapter Thirty-Five         Meeting the Owner       229
Chapter Thirty-Six          A New Man               237
Chapter Thirty-Seven        Sharehouse Meeting      245
Chapter Thirty-Eight        Changed Hearts!         251

*What Would Jesus Do?*

Copyright © 1997 by Questar Publications
Illustrations, © 1997 by Kip Richmond

ISBN: 1-57673-053-0

Contents based on material from:
What Would Jesus Do? © 1991 by Questar Publishers, Inc.
In His Hands © 1993 by Questar Publishers, Inc.

What Would Jesus Do? was previously published by Gold and Honey, a division of Multnomah
Publishers

Design: David Haidle
Editorial: Jeanne Taylor and Barbara Martin

Most scripture quotations are from: The Contemporary English Version, © 1995 by American
Bible Society. Also quoted: The King James Version, © by Thomas Nelson, Inc.

Zonder**kidz**
The Children's Group of ZondervanPublishingHouse

Grand Rapids, Michigan 49530
www.zonderkidz.com

Zonderkidz is a trademark of the Zondervan Corporation

*Printed in the United States of America*

00 01 02 03 04 05 06 / 19  18  17  16  15  14

# PICNIC STRANGER

## Chapter One

"You're it!" Claire laughed, tagging Bill on the shoulder.

"Not for long!" Bill yelled as he chased her. Claire dashed around the picnic tables, her long curls flying.

Giggles and laughter filled the air as the children played tag in the field beside the church. It was the Bible School summer picnic. Everyone from Pine Ridge had gathered in the churchyard.

Men roasted chickens over the fire pit while ladies sliced strawberry pie and prepared salads. Several older girls gathered bouquets of wildflowers and took care of the toddlers. In the field behind the church, young men organized a game of softball.

"Lunch will be ready soon," Parson Henry said to the children. "If you go into the woods, be sure to listen for our call."

Claire ran over and gave him a quick hug. "I'll come when you call, Papa," she said with a smile.

"Come on," hollered Bill. "Let's hunt for pine cones!"

All the boys and girls scampered into the woods except for Claire and Bill, who stopped to grab a bucket for their cones. When Claire ran toward the edge of the woods, she caught sight of a dirty-faced boy running down the road in front of the church.

"Bill, who is that boy?" asked Claire.

"I've never seen him before," said Bill, "but he looks like he's crying."

Claire and Bill ducked behind the bushes so the boy wouldn't see them. They watched him hurry across the field toward the churchyard.

"Listen!" Claire whispered to Bill. "He's talking to himself."

The dirty-faced boy prayed out loud as he walked. "Dear Jesus, please show me someone who will help me—just as you would if you were here."

Claire and Bill saw the boy walk up to the men who were slicing the roasted chicken.

"Can you please help me?" he asked. "My hands are all scraped up and my friend needs help."

"We're busy fixing the meat," said one of the men. "Go ask the ladies."

The boy went over to the picnic tables and held up his scraped and dirty hands. "Could you please help me?" he asked. "And I have a friend who needs help."

"Waaaaaah! Waaaaaaah!" cried a toddler who had fallen into a mud puddle.

"We're sorry," said a lady who was holding a pair of twins. "Our little ones need to be washed and fed right now."

"Please run along until later," said another woman carrying a tiny baby.

"Everyone is so busy," Bill said to Claire. "They don't understand. That boy needs help!"

"Somebody needs to help him," said Claire. "Should *we*?"

"We don't even know him," said Bill. "Besides, we're too young to help."

Do you think that you are too young to help others? Why or why not?

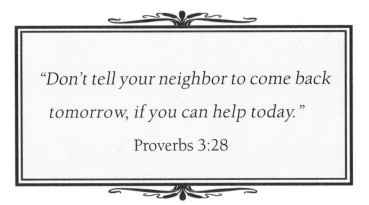

*"Don't tell your neighbor to come back tomorrow, if you can help today."*
Proverbs 3:28

# THE PROBLEM

## Chapter Two

The dirty-faced stranger ran over to the boys playing ball, but they were in the middle of a game and didn't have time for him. He walked to a tree stump nearby and sat on it. Tears rolled down his cheeks.

Claire peeked out from behind a tree. "Nobody will listen to him," she whispered to Bill.

"Shh!" Bill said. He cocked his head toward the woods. The sound of children singing a happy song could be heard through the trees.

We have decided to follow Jesus,

We have decided to follow Jesus,

We have decided to follow Jesus,

In every way, through every day.

"Lunch is ready!" called Parson Henry. Boys and
girls ran out of the woods, carrying their pine cones.
But Claire and Bill stayed behind the tree. They took
another look at the young stranger.

"He is very dirty," whispered Claire. "And his clothes are ripped."

"He looks hurt," Bill said quietly.

Claire looked at the crowd gathering around the picnic table full of food.

Parson Henry called toward the woods, "Claire! Please come. It's time to eat!"

"Daddy's calling me. I'd better go," she said.

"Let's run!" said Bill. "I don't want to be at the end of the line!"

As they ran past the dirty-faced boy, he called to them. "Please wait!"

Bill and Claire stopped and looked back at the boy.

"I heard someone singing about Jesus," he said. "Do you know Jesus?"

"Yes." They nodded their heads.

"I know Jesus, too. I wonder if the people at the picnic know Jesus. If they do, why didn't they help me? I only wanted some water for my scratched hands and some help for my friend who is in trouble."

Claire was silent. She didn't know what to say. Neither did Bill.

Suddenly a dog barked in the distance. The boy stood up quickly. "That's Murphy!" he said. "I need to get back to my friend!" Then he turned and ran back to the road.

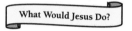
What Would Jesus Do?

What do you think Jesus wants you to do for other people in your family? Your school? Your neighborhood?

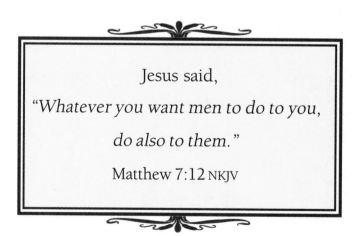

Jesus said,
*"Whatever you want men to do to you,*
*do also to them."*
Matthew 7:12 NKJV

# HARD QUESTIONS

## Chapter Three

Claire watched the young stranger hurry out of sight. "Jesus loves everyone. Jesus would help that boy," she said. "What could *we* do to help?"

"I don't know," said Bill. "But let's ask your father. Right now!" He grabbed Claire by the hand and they ran to the picnic crowd.

Bill and Claire hurried to the picnic table. "Parson Henry," said Bill. "We need your help. I mean, that boy needs your help."

Parson Henry looked bewildered.

"Did you see that dirty-faced boy, Papa?" asked Claire.

"No, I didn't," her father answered.

"He was hurt and his friend needed help," said Claire. "Wouldn't Jesus want us to help him?"

Parson Henry nodded. "Oh, yes! Jesus always helped everyone who came to him. When people needed help, Jesus took time out for them. Remember our Bible lesson last week about the blind beggar sitting beside the road?"

Claire's eyes lit up. "Was he the man who kept shouting for Jesus?" she asked. "Even when other people told him to be quiet?"

Her father smiled and nodded.

"I remember that story," said Bill. "Jesus took time to heal the blind man's eyes." Bill thought for a moment. "Nobody took time to help the boy who came to our picnic."

"He asked for help," said Claire. "Isn't every child important to God? Shouldn't we help him?"

"Of course!" said her father. "And we will go right away to help that boy. Bill, see if your mother brought an extra shirt for you today. Claire, you grab a bar of soap. I hope we can still catch up with him."

After Parson Henry pumped some water into a bucket, he and the two children hurried down the hill in search of the boy.

**What Would Jesus Do?**

It always takes time to help people. When have you spent time helping others?

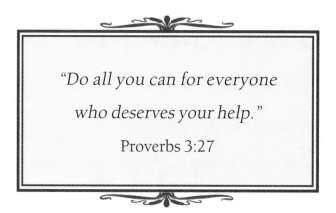

*"Do all you can for everyone*

*who deserves your help."*

Proverbs 3:27

To learn more about the blind beggar and Jesus, read Luke 18:35-43.

# TAKING TIME

## Chapter Four

As Bill ran down the cobblestone road, water splashed out of the bucket and down his pant leg.

Claire raced ahead of her father and Bill as they hurried to catch up with the dirty-faced boy. Past the bridge, at the top of a hill, she saw the boy up ahead.

"There he is!" she called to Bill and her father.

"Wait for us!" Claire called out to the young stranger.

The boy turned when he heard Claire. He stopped in the middle of the road and waited for the three of them to run up the hill.

They handed him the clean shirt, soap, and bucket of water. "Who are you?" asked Parson Henry.

"I'm Jack Browning," he said quietly. They told him their names and helped him wash up.

"My friend needs help, too," said Jack. "Listen! Do you hear his dog, Murphy?"

"How can we help your friend?" asked Parson Henry.

"Follow me. I'll take you to him," said Jack. As they reached the top of the hill, Jack pointed to an old man sitting on a log beside the road. "My friend is blind. He can't get around without his cane. While we were walking today, he tripped and fell. His cane rolled into that gully full of blackberry bushes."

Jack continued, "I climbed down and tried to get the cane, but I slipped and fell on the rocks."

The elderly blind man cocked his head toward the road and called, "Jack! Welcome back! Who's with you?"

Jack ran over to the old man. "These are my new friends: Bill, Claire, and Parson Henry. They helped me wash up and gave me a new shirt. And they want to help you, Mr. Martin."

The blind man smiled. "This reminds me of a story in the Bible when Jesus' friends ate dinner together. Their feet were dirty from the dusty roads, but nobody wanted to wash anyone else's feet. Do you children know what Jesus did?"

"Yes," said Claire. "Jesus washed everyone's feet!"

"That's right," Mr. Martin said. "And Jesus told his friends, 'This is my example: Help one another, just as I help you; serve one another, just as I serve you.'" The old man held out his hand. "I want to thank you for helping Jack, just like Jesus would!"

Claire looked down at her shoes while Parson Henry coughed. "I'm sorry we waited so long to help Jack," he explained as he shook Mr. Martin's hand.

Mr. Martin nodded. "I understand. It's not always easy to do as Jesus would do."

"What should we do now?" asked Bill.

"Well," Claire said with a grin. "What would Jesus do?"

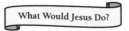
What Would Jesus Do?

What would Jesus do to help others in your family?
How can you help someone today?

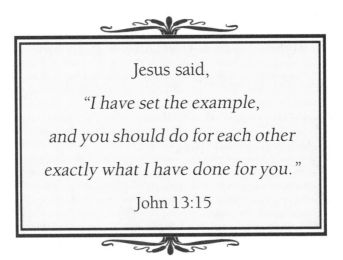

Jesus said,

*"I have set the example,*

*and you should do for each other*

*exactly what I have done for you."*

John 13:15

Read about Jesus washing his disciples' feet in John 13:1-17.

# NEW FRIENDS

## Chapter Five

Claire and Bill walked over to the edge of the gully beside the road.

"Look at all those jagged rocks," said Claire. "I wouldn't want to go down that steep gully. I know I would fall into the blackberry stickers."

"Look!" said Bill. "I see the tip of Mr. Martin's cane near the bottom of the gully, under the thorns."

"It will be hard to get that cane," said Claire. "But I know Jesus wants us to work together. Let's help Jack."

Everyone formed a chain. Parson Henry held onto Claire, and Claire held Bill's hand while Bill hung onto Jack's hand. Then Jack carefully climbed over the sharp rocks, down, down, down the steep sides. When Jack reached the bottom of the gully, he carefully lifted the thorny blackberry vines and grabbed the lost cane.

Then everyone helped pull Jack back up the slope and onto the road.

"Here, Mr. Martin," Jack said, placing the cane in the blind man's hand. "This is from *all* of us. I couldn't have gotten your cane without the help of our new friends."

"Thank you!" said Mr. Martin. "Thanks to each one of you!" He stood up and shook hands with all of them. "My dear friends, I hope you will always remember to ask these four special words: *What would Jesus do?*"

"We will!" said Claire and Bill.

"We are glad we met both of you," said Parson Henry. "And we would like to share our picnic with you. Isn't that what Jesus would do? Can you come back to the church with us?"

Jack tipped his cap to them. "Thank you for inviting us, but we have been gone too long. We need to return home." He smiled at Claire and Bill. "Now don't forget those four special words."

Mr. Martin stood up to leave. "I will be praying for all of you," he said. "Jack and I walk this way every afternoon. Please meet us here again, and let us know what happens."

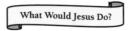

What Would Jesus Do?

When have you worked hard for someone? Did you complain? Did you work cheerfully?

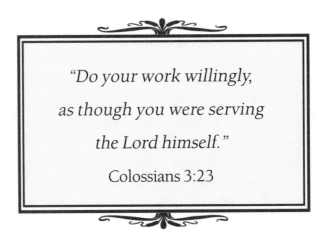

*"Do your work willingly,*

*as though you were serving*

*the Lord himself."*

Colossians 3:23

# HIGH HOPES

## Chapter Six

Claire skipped ahead of Bill and her father as they crossed the bridge and headed back to the picnic.

"Let's hurry!" she said. "I want to tell my friends what I have learned today. I just know they will want to learn those four special words."

"I hope they will," said Parson Henry.

"Of course they will!" said Claire. "They all love Jesus. They will all want to ask, *What would Jesus do?*"

When they arrived back at the church, Claire and Bill quickly filled their plates and went to the table where the other children were eating.

Parson Henry came and sat down beside Claire. He looked around the table and said, "I enjoyed hearing you children sing *I Have Decided to Follow Jesus.* And I'm sure you understand that we don't just *sing* about following Jesus. Following him is something we *do* every day."

"That's right!" said Bill. "Jesus wants us to love and help other people, like the dirty-faced boy who came to our picnic and asked for help. We are glad we went to help him and his blind friend."

"The blind man told us about a new plan," Claire explained to her friends while they ate strawberry pie. "Every day, when Bill and I are playing or working, we want to remember to ask ourselves a special question: *What would Jesus do?* And we'll pray to Jesus. He will help us know what to do."

Nobody looked up at Claire. They were all too busy eating. Claire picked at her food. Nothing seemed to taste very good. She noticed that Bill had stopped eating, too. "Will any of you try asking this question with us?" said Claire, looking around the table.

"Maybe later," replied a boy with freckles. "First we want to play." He jumped up and yelled to the others, "Last one to the old stump is it!"

Claire propped her elbows on the picnic table and watched the other children play. She blinked hard, holding back her tears.

What Would Jesus Do?

How can you show Jesus that you want to follow him?

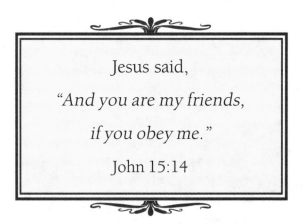

Jesus said,

*"And you are my friends,*

*if you obey me."*

John 15:14

Read Matthew 4:18-22 and 9:9 to find out what happened when Jesus invited people to follow him.

# BIG DECISIONS

## Chapter Seven

Claire and Bill didn't feel like playing games anymore. They sat silently at the picnic table, watching the other children play tag.

Finally Claire stood up and walked back to her house beside the church. She went inside and got her jump rope. Winding the jump rope around her hand, she walked slowly back to the table where her father and Bill sat talking.

Bill shook his head sadly and said, "It's no use, Parson Henry. Nobody seems interested in asking, *What would Jesus do?* Maybe it's not a good idea."

Claire stood nearby, holding her jump rope. She heard her father say, "Even if no one joins us, we will still follow Jesus. This is not your idea, Bill. And it's not mine. It was *Jesus* who asked his friends to follow his example."

"That's right!" Bill said. "This is Jesus' idea, not ours. I think that's why we met Mr. Martin and Jack, so Jesus could teach us to do what he would do."

Standing up tall, Bill stated, "I will follow Jesus!"

"You're talking like Peter in the Bible!" said Parson Henry with a twinkle in his eye. "I'm glad you want to be one of Jesus' disciples. Just remember, it is easy to *say* that you want to be like Jesus. The hard part is *doing* it!"

"I will try this week," said Bill. "When anything happens, I will ask the question: *What would Jesus do?*"

Parson Henry stood up next to Bill. "So will I!"

Claire swallowed a lump in her throat. "Me, too," she said, laying her jump rope on the table.

The three partners joined hands and prayed. Then they sang their promise to one another:

*We have decided to follow Jesus;*

*We have decided to follow Jesus;*

*We have decided to follow Jesus;*

*We'll be like him. We'll be like him.*

Everyone left the picnic as a chilly wind blew across the field. Claire looked up at the darkening sky. Gray and purple clouds moved across the setting sun.

"It has been a good day," said her father, glancing at the clouds. "But it looks like a bad storm is brewing."

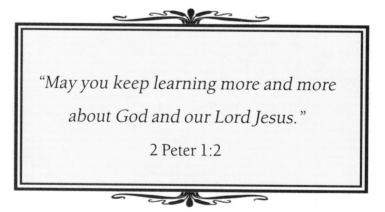

What Would Jesus Do?

Think about a time when you wanted to follow Jesus, but someone else didn't.

Are you willing to do what Jesus says, even when others won't?

*"May you keep learning more and more about God and our Lord Jesus."*

2 Peter 1:2

# STORMY NIGHT

## Chapter Eight

A few hours later, Bill climbed into his bed. Lightning flashed and each thunder blast sounded louder than the last.

*CRACK! BA-BOOM!*

Bill burrowed under the covers and tried to shut out the sound of the storm.

Wind and rain pounded on the
window pane. Bill pulled the pillow
over his head. "I don't like storms!
I'm afraid!" he cried.

The storm thundered back.

*CRACK! BA-BOOMMM! Rumble-brummm!*

Bill grabbed his pillow, tumbled to the floor,

and rolled under the bed.

*CRACK! BA-BOOMMM! Rumble-brum-brummm!*

Squeezing a little farther under his bed, Bill felt something beside him. It was the picture Bible that Parson Henry had given him for his birthday!

Bill thought about Claire and her father. And then he remembered the four special words: *What would Jesus do?* Right there under his bed, Bill prayed. "Dear Jesus, please help me. What would you do in this storm? Would you be afraid?"

As the lightning flashed, Bill looked in his Bible. He found a picture of Jesus on a boat in the middle of a stormy lake. Jesus' friends in the boat looked scared. Bill knew that story. He remembered that Jesus had said, "Don't be afraid!" And then the storm stopped and the wind and waves were still.

*CRACK! BA-BOOM!*

The sound echoed around Bill's room.

*Rumble-brum-brummm!*

Bill closed his eyes and prayed, "Thank you, Jesus. I know that you love me. I don't have to be afraid when you are here with me." Then Bill climbed back into his bed and fell fast asleep.

What Would Jesus Do?

When do you feel scared?

What could you tell someone who is afraid?

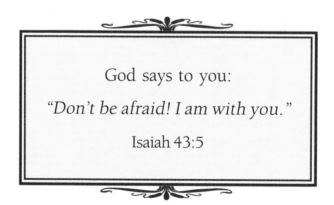

God says to you:

*"Don't be afraid! I am with you."*

Isaiah 43:5

To find out more about how Jesus stopped the storm, read Matthew 8:23-27.

# A LOST JUMP ROPE

## Chapter Nine

I'm going to jump rope all day!" Claire told her father when she came to breakfast the next morning. "My beautiful jump rope is the best birthday present I've ever had."

Her father smiled as he handed Claire a bowl of oatmeal. "I knew you would enjoy it. You waited a long time for a jump rope."

After she had eaten breakfast, Claire rushed to her bedroom to get the jump rope. It wasn't there. She ran outside and looked in the backyard. It wasn't there.

Claire searched all over the barn. But it wasn't there either. She couldn't find it anywhere! Suddenly she remembered. "The picnic table by the church. *That's* where I left it!"

Claire ran over to the churchyard. Little Jordan
and Michael McCree were playing with something in
the dirt. It was her jump rope! Claire wanted to run
over and grab it away from them. She wanted to
scream, "Leave my birthday jump rope alone!" Then
she remembered those four special words: *"What
would Jesus do?"*

Claire stopped behind the tree and prayed, "If this jump rope belonged to you, Jesus, what would *you* do?" She remembered the Bible story when Jesus fed many people because one boy shared his lunch.

"Oh, Jesus," she whispered. "You gave me this jump rope. Help me to share it with these little boys." Instead of taking her jump rope away, she walked over to the youngsters and joined their game.

Claire's jump rope soon became a corral for their pets.

And a line to catch fish in the sea.

And the reins for a team of reindeer.

At lunchtime, the boys left for home. "Good bye, Claire!" they called. "Thanks for sharing your jump rope. We had lots of fun!"

"Thank *you*, Jesus, for the happy time," whispered Claire as she skipped rope all the way home.

What do you find hardest to share with others?

What do you think Jesus would want you to share?

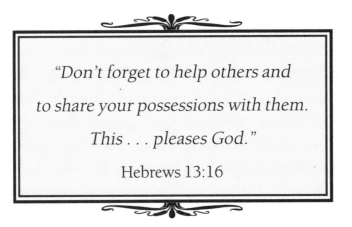

> *"Don't forget to help others and*
> *to share your possessions with them.*
> *This . . . pleases God."*
>
> Hebrews 13:16

To learn about what happened when a widow shared her food with a prophet named Elijah, read 1 Kings 17:8-15.

# COAL VALLEY NEIGHBORS

## Chapter Ten

Claire knocked politely at the church office door. *Tap-tap-tap.* "My father is probably studying for his sermon," she told Bill, who stood patiently beside her.

"Come in," called Parson Henry.

Claire pushed the door open, ran around the desk, and gave her father a hug. Bill stepped inside the office.

"Hi, Papa!" said Claire. "Bill and I want to read about what Jesus said and did. Can you tell us where to look in our Bibles?"

"Start reading the Gospel of Matthew," said Parson Henry. "Then read Mark, Luke, and John."

A knock at the door interrupted them. They turned to see the children's Bible teacher standing by the open door and wiping her eyes.

"Good afternoon, Miss Emily!" said Parson Henry. "Say, are you all right? Are those tears I see?"

She answered softly, "I rode my horse down to Coal Valley today. It was the first time I've ever been there. What I saw made me cry. Those old houses are very dirty and run-down. I don't know how anyone lives in them! And the people are so poor. Their children don't even have shoes."

"I've never been to the old mining town," admitted Parson Henry. "I knew some people stayed there after the mine shut down, but I didn't know what happened to them."

"Is there something we can do for them?" asked Miss Emily.

Bill and Claire both spoke up at once: *"The four special words!"*

Miss Emily didn't understand, so Claire told her about the events of the past two days.

"Bill and I want to follow Jesus," said Claire. "Here's a chance to ask, *What would Jesus do?*"

Parson Henry's eyes looked thoughtful. "Remember the story Jesus told about the Good Samaritan?" he asked. "Well, people in Coal Valley are neighbors to us. Jesus would want us to help them, especially if they are poor and not well."

"Can we have another picnic and invite them?" asked Claire.

"And give them some of our shoes?" added Bill.

Miss Emily glanced at Parson Henry and said, "I am not sure what our church members would say."

Claire said, "I've heard some people say we should stay away from Coal Valley."

"Hmm." Parson Henry frowned. "Our members might not be ready for this idea. And I think it's too soon to organize another picnic right now."

Just then, barking and neighing sounded outside.

Everyone rushed to the
window and looked out. They saw two dogs
chasing a cat around the churchyard. The cat
dashed underneath Sugarbelle, Miss Emily's horse.

Sugarbelle kicked and reared until her reins broke loose. Then she took off running. Parson Henry dashed out of his office and followed Sugarbelle across the field. "I'll catch her!" he shouted.

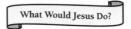

What Would Jesus Do?

Who are your "neighbors"?
What can you do to be a good neighbor?

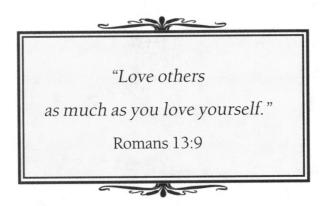

*"Love others*

*as much as you love yourself."*

Romans 13:9

To learn about the Good Samaritan, read Luke 10:25-37.

# A REMINDER

## Chapter Eleven

I'm coming, too!" Claire yelled, racing after her father and the runaway horse. She ran as fast as she could until her cheeks felt like they were on fire and her lungs felt like they would burst. She struggled to keep up with her father as he chased Miss Emily's horse through the nearby field.

Bill sprinted ahead of Claire as they climbed the steep hillside.

"Whoa!" Parson Henry yelled. "Sugarbelle! STOP!"

As Bill and Claire followed Parson Henry and Sugarbelle over the hill, they saw the horse running down the road straight toward their friends, Jack and Mr. Martin! When Jack saw the runaway horse, he wasn't afraid. He quickly reached out, grabbed the reins, and pulled the horse to a stop.

When Claire got close to Jack and the horse, she heard him speaking quietly to Sugarbelle.

*"Neighhhh!"* snorted Sugarbelle, standing at Jack's side and pawing the ground.

Parson Henry was relieved. "Thanks for hanging onto those reins, Jack," he said.

"I'm glad to help!" said Jack. "I was walking with Mr. Martin and listening to some of his favorite Bible stories. I'm so glad that Jesus loves *everyone:* rich people and poor people, clean people and dirty people, well people and sick people."

Claire watched her father put one arm around Jack's shoulder and the other around Mr. Martin's.

"I want to be like Jesus and I know you both do, too," said Parson Henry. "I am thankful we can love each other...like Jesus loves each of us. Thank you, Jack, for reminding me of this."

"Now we must go and do some planning for a picnic," said Parson Henry, taking Sugarbelle's reins. "I want to remember to ask what Jesus would do."

Claire silently held her father's hand as he led Sugarbelle down the hill. She knew he was thinking about Jack's words.

Miss Emily stood by the road waiting for them. They gave the horse back to her, then Parson Henry invited them to join hands and pray.

"We're sorry, Jesus," said Parson Henry. "It's easier to think about what others would say instead of what you would say. Help us do what you want us to do."

"Now let's get that picnic planned!" said Parson Henry as they headed back to the church.

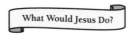

What Would Jesus Do?

Can you think of some children who don't have many friends? What would Jesus do for them?

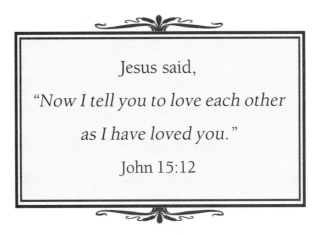

Jesus said,

*"Now I tell you to love each other*

*as I have loved you."*

John 15:12

To find out how Jesus treated a man named Zacchaeus, read Luke 19:1-10.

## CLAIRE'S DECISION

### Chapter Twelve

Later that same afternoon, Claire skipped rope down the road, hoping to find a playmate.

"Hello, Claire," called a voice behind her.

Claire turned to see her teacher riding Sugarbelle.

"Hi, Miss Emily! Where are you going now?"

Miss Emily flashed a smile as she rode up beside Claire. "I am busy getting the food and the games organized for our big picnic next Sunday afternoon. But first I'm going to ride down to Coal Valley to invite everyone to come and join us," she said.

Claire's eyes sparkled. "I'll help make baked beans and corn bread for our guests," she said. "And I'll bring one of my dresses for another girl."

"That is a wonderful idea, Claire! I hope each boy and girl at church will bring a nice piece of clothing to the picnic. I also want to ask everyone to bring a special gift for a child from Coal Valley. It could be a favorite toy or something else you like. Those children don't have any toys at all."

Watching her teacher ride away, Claire twirled and jumped rope, keeping time with her skips. She made up a song as she thought about what Miss Emily had said: *Every girl...every boy...bring a gift...a favorite toy....*

Claire smiled. "Every child would *love* to have a jump rope!" Suddenly she stopped skipping. Looking at her jump rope, she frowned. "Wait a minute! Surely Miss Emily doesn't mean my jump rope! I got that jump rope for my birthday. I don't have to give it away!"

Claire sighed and sat down in the grass. Somehow she didn't feel like jumping rope anymore. "Oh, what should I do? I don't want someone else to have my jump rope," she said to a squirrel perched in the tree. "I could pretend to be sick and stay home from the picnic. Or I could hide my rope and say it was lost."

But Claire knew it would not be right to lie.

She almost started to pray. And she *almost* said those four special words. But she was afraid to ask what Jesus would want her to do. Instead, Claire scrambled to her feet and skipped rope down the path as fast as she could.

"It's *my* jump rope and I want to keep it!" She gripped the shiny red handles tighter than ever. "I am *not* going to give it away!"

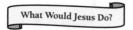

What Would Jesus Do?

Take time to ask Jesus how you can share. What are you willing to share with others?

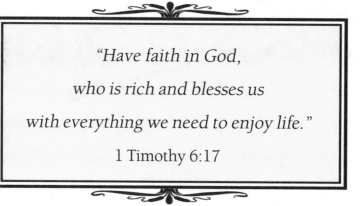

*"Have faith in God,*

*who is rich and blesses us*

*with everything we need to enjoy life."*

1 Timothy 6:17

To learn about a boy who shared, read Matthew 14:13-21.

# CLAIRE'S FEAR

## Chapter Thirteen

While Claire was jumping rope down the road, she suddenly heard a voice calling to her. "Hello, Claire!"

Up ahead she saw Jack, Mr. Martin, and his dog, Murphy, resting underneath the shady trees beside the road. Claire jumped her rope up to them and sat down in the cool grass.

"There is going to be a big picnic next Sunday!"
Jack said. "Miss Emily rode by and told us about it."

"Yes, I know," said Claire. "Miss Emily is asking all
of us kids to bring something to give a Coal Valley
child. But I know she doesn't mean my jump rope.
I am not giving *that* away," Claire stated firmly.

"Claire," Mr. Martin said quietly.

"Have you asked, *What would Jesus do?*"

Claire didn't answer. Tears filled her eyes. "But I don't *want* to ask that question," she said. "I'm afraid Jesus would make me give away my jump rope."

Mr. Martin nodded his head. "I understand how you feel, Claire, and Jesus understands, too."

Claire was thankful that Jack looked away. She felt ready to burst into tears. Murphy licked her hand while she leaned her hot face against his back.

"I would like to go on a treasure hunt," said Mr. Martin. "Let's find some treasures God made for us. Jack, can you lead me down the path to the creek? Claire, why don't you come along with us?"

Mr. Martin and Jack got up and headed down the path toward the nearby creek. Claire and Murphy followed close behind them.

**What Would Jesus Do?**

Have there been times that someone didn't share what they had with you?

What do you find is the hardest to *share*?

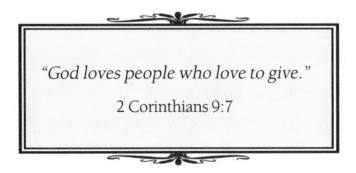

*"God loves people who love to give."*

2 Corinthians 9:7

To find out who gave God the best gift, read Luke 21:1-4.

# FINDING TREASURE

## Chapter Fourteen

S ince I am blind," said Mr. Martin to Claire, "you must help me find God's treasures. Tell me what you see as we walk."

Claire looked around the meadow and nearby woods. "A bright sun is shining," she said. "And the clear blue sky is full of puffy clouds. Lots of pretty butterflies are flapping around the fields of wild-flowers."

Stopping at the edge of the creek, Mr. Martin and the children sat down in the grass. After they pulled off their shoes and socks, they dangled their feet in the cold water.

"What does it look like here?" Mr. Martin asked.

"Sunshine streams through the trees and sparkles on the water," said Claire. "The creek is full of mossy rocks." She picked up a rock and placed it in his hand. "Feel how soft the moss is. It has different shades of green with little specks of red in it."

Jack reached over and picked some dandelions.

"Rub these flowers against your nose, Mr. Martin," he

said with a laugh. "They tickle!"

Mr. Martin rubbed the petals across his nose and cheek. "I like how soft and velvety they feel," he said with a smile. "Now, if you listen, I will share my treasures with you."

The children held very still.

"Because I am blind, I have trained my ears to collect treasures," said Mr. Martin. "Do you hear the wind blowing through the treetops and the water bubbling over the stones in the creek?" he asked.

Mr. Martin cocked his head. "Listen! Can you hear the sparrows chirping and bullfrogs croaking? Everything I hear is a treasure from God to enjoy. Now look at the three of us. What do you see?"

Claire wiggled her toes in the water and said, "I see a blind man with a girl and boy."

"Do you know what Jesus sees?" he asked.

"What?" asked Claire.

"Jesus sees three *treasures*! He made us and he loves us. And he willingly gave his life on the cross for us. We are valuable treasures to him!" Mr. Martin reached out his arms and hugged the children.

"I feel you are each a treasure to me!" he said.
"And now I want to make sure you know about the
*greatest* treasure of all."

What Would Jesus Do?

What "treasure" has God given to you?
Which "treasures" from God do you enjoy the most?

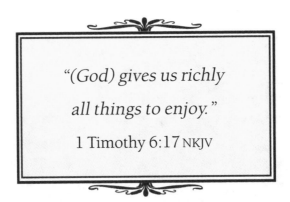
"*(God) gives us richly
all things to enjoy.*"
1 Timothy 6:17 NKJV

# THE GREATEST TREASURE

## Chapter Fifteen

ooking across the sparkling creek, Claire watched the birds and butterflies flying in the meadow. "God made lots of treasures for us," she said. "Which is the greatest?"

"Well," said Mr. Martin. "If you want to find God's greatest treasure, you must open up God's special treasure chest. Do you know what that is?"

"Is it the Bible?" asked Claire.

"Yes. The Bible is a treasure chest. In it you will find the world's greatest treasure," he said.

"I read about Jesus in the Bible," said Claire. "Is he the greatest treasure?"

Mr. Martin smiled. "Yes, he is. Jesus loves us. When he died for us on the cross, he gave us the greatest gift anyone could give—he gave his life."

Claire silently looked down at her jump rope.

"Do you think Jesus feels unhappy because he gave us so much?" asked Mr. Martin. "Do you think he feels sad?"

"Oh, no," Claire answered. "I think he is happy because he loves us."

"Yes," said Mr. Martin. "Can you feel his smile in the sunshine and hear his laughter in the breeze? If you are very quiet, you can hear Jesus whispering his love in your heart."

"I want to know Jesus better," said Jack.

"So do I," said Claire. As she thought about how much Jesus loved her, a tear rolled down each cheek.

"When you read your Bible and talk to Jesus every day, you will learn about him and come to know him," said Mr. Martin.

"And then we will know what Jesus would do," added Jack.

The sun soaked into Claire and warmed her deep inside. She lay back in the grass and listened to the bubbling stream and singing birds. Finally she leaned forward and tugged on the old man's sleeve. "Mr. Martin," Claire whispered. "I'd like to pray."

"Go ahead, dear," he said softly.

"Dear Jesus, please forgive me for being selfish," she prayed. "Thank you for giving your life for me. Now I can give away my birthday jump rope. It won't make me sad. You're still glad, even though you gave everything. Help me do what you would do. Amen."

"You know," said Mr. Martin later as he and Jack walked Claire home, "giving your jump rope to the Coal Valley children will bring you much joy. Just wait and see!"

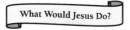
**What Would Jesus Do?**

What did Jesus give up for you?

How can you get to know Jesus better?

> *"Our Lord Jesus Christ was kind enough to give up all his riches and become poor, so that you could become rich."*
>
> 2 Corinthians 8:9

# TROUBLE TIME

## Chapter Sixteen

On Saturday afternoon, Claire followed Bill deep into the woods, chasing blue jays and squirrels.

Suddenly Bill stopped. "Get down!" he whispered as he quickly crouched behind a bush. Claire knew something was wrong. She hurriedly squatted beside him and peeked out through the bushes.

"Look!" whispered Bill. "Some boys are over there, by the shed under the oak trees."

Then Claire saw them. It was Casey, Dan, and Travis, three of the school's biggest troublemakers!

"Oh, Bill!" she said. "The one wearing the red cap is Dan Roper. He pesters all the little kids at recess."

"Shh!" whispered Bill. "Let's find out what they are doing. That's probably their hideout."

"Let's leave!" urged Claire.

"No!" said Bill, creeping closer. "I want to hear what they are saying. Be quiet and listen!"

Claire heard Casey Larsen talking. "I want to go early to the picnic next Sunday and get the best food!"

"Forget it, Casey," said Dan. "I don't want to be around all those people from Coal Valley. There's gotta be something more exciting around here than a church picnic. I'd like to see a fight, or a train wreck, or a blazing fire!"

"Hey, we could visit that old mining town while everyone else is at the picnic," said Travis.

"Why would you want to go there?" asked Casey.

"To have a little fun!" Travis said with a mischievious grin. "We can take along our matches and play a little *trick*."

Casey spoke up loudly. "What's the matter with you? Matches can start a fire! What if you burn something down?"

"But this is just for *fun*," said Travis. "We won't hurt anyone. Even if a fire started, it wouldn't ruin much. Those old houses are nothing but shacks."

Claire yanked on Bill's sleeve. "We'd better get out of here fast!" she said. Just then, she saw Bill's nose begin to twitch. She cringed as Bill covered his nose with his hand, but he was too late.

"Uh, uh, uh, UH-CHOO!" he sneezed.

Claire scrunched down as small as she could and squeezed her eyes shut. When she looked up again, the three bullies were staring down at her and Bill.

What Would Jesus Do?

What are some things you can do when someone else wants to make trouble or hurt others?

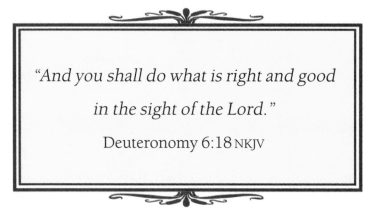

*"And you shall do what is right and good in the sight of the Lord."*

Deuteronomy 6:18 NKJV

# THE WARNING

## Chapter Seventeen

Claire wanted to run away, but her legs felt too weak to stand. She grabbed Bill's arm and tried to keep from shaking with fear.

Dan glared down at the two children. "You kids heard our plan, didn't you? Don't you dare tell anyone. If you do, we'll throw you down the old mine shaft by our hideout!"

Travis said, "Yeah, it's scary down there. The creepy spiders grow bigger than your hand!" He stuck his huge hands in front of their faces and wiggled his fingers.

"Ten-foot-long poisonous snakes live there, too!" said Casey.

"And grizzly bears hibernate in the mine," said Dan. "That's where we'll put you two if you tell anyone our plans. Do you understand?"

Bill's teeth chattered as he nodded his head. Claire couldn't say anything as she burst into tears.

"Get out of here!" the boys shouted. "And *never* ever come back!"

The children jumped up and ran away as fast as they could. "Where are we going?" Claire yelled to Bill as they dashed through the woods.

"Find Jack...and Mr. Martin," he gasped. "Head for the road...where they walk."

The children ran down the hill toward the road. The boys' voices laughed and echoed through the trees behind them.

"Remember those spiders and snakes and wild bears!" hollered the boys. "You will never get out of the mine shaft alive!"

Claire and Bill were so scared! They didn't remember
to ask the four special words. All they wanted to do
was run away. They were even too scared to look for
Jack and Mr. Martin.

Both Claire and Bill forgot to stop and ask Jesus to help them be brave. They just ran as fast as they could and never once looked back.

What Would Jesus Do?

Can you think of a time when you were scared by what others said or did? What happened?

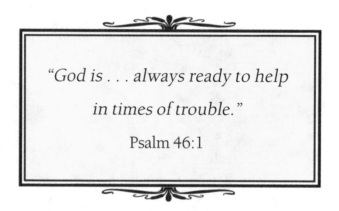

*"God is . . . always ready to help in times of trouble."*

Psalm 46:1

Find out how soldiers felt when they faced their biggest enemy. Discover who was the bravest. Read 1 Samuel 17.

# A CHANCE TO TELL

## Chapter Eighteen

Finally the frightened children reached the churchyard. Their hearts were pounding as they ran around the corner of the church building. *Whammm!* They crashed headfirst into Parson Henry who had just stepped out of his office. They all fell on top of each other in a heap on the grass.

"Whoa!" said Parson Henry. He struggled to sit up. "What's your hurry? Where are you two going?"

Bill stood up and brushed himself off. "We were trying to get away from the woods," he said. "Away from spiders as big as your hand!"

"We don't have any spiders like that around here," said Parson Henry. "Is that why you're scared?"

"I'm not scared," said Bill, glancing back toward the woods. "I'm just worried about spiders getting in Claire's long hair."

Claire's cheeks felt red and hot. "Daddy, what about poisonous snakes?" she asked. "Have you ever seen any? Do they bite people?"

"There aren't any poisonous snakes close by, Claire. Don't worry. Just stay away from the dark crevices between the rocks by the old mine. Snakes usually hide in dark places."

"Have you ever been in a really dark place, Parson Henry?" asked Bill.

Parson Henry laughed. "Oh, yes! I was in the church storm cellar once during the darkest storm I've ever known. But I remembered that Jesus said, 'I am the Light of the world. Whoever follows me will never walk in darkness.'" He put his arms around Claire and Bill. "No matter how dark it seems, Jesus is always with us. We can trust him."

Claire nodded and tried to smile.

"Parson Henry," said Bill, "do we know anyone who lives in Coal Valley?"

"Not yet. We'll meet them at tomorrow's picnic."

As it began to rain, Parson Henry held open his office door and urged, "Come in and get out of the rain."

"I need to go home," said Bill. He ran off while Claire dashed over to the house.

What Would Jesus Do?

Have you ever had a problem that seemed too big for God? Did you ask God for help?

*"God is our mighty fortress, always ready to help in times of trouble."*

Psalm 46:1

Read how God helped sailors during a storm in Acts 27.

# COAL VALLEY SURPRISE

## Chapter Nineteen

Claire tossed and turned all night. When she came down for breakfast, she couldn't help wondering what would happen that afternoon at the church picnic and at the old mining town.

"What a sunny day for our picnic!" said Parson Henry as he headed out the kitchen door. "I'm going to the office to get everything ready for church." He stopped and looked back at his daughter. She silently stirred her cereal around in the bowl.

"Do you feel okay, Claire?" he asked. "Are you still going to help this afternoon with the gunny sack races?"

"Yes, I'll help," she said, trying to smile at her father. "I'm just tired."

After her father left, Claire put the breakfast dishes in the sink, got her Bible, and then walked slowly to the church. She found a seat where she could sit alone in the back of the classroom.

When Bill arrived, he came and sat down beside Claire. They didn't say anything to each other.

Claire stared out the window while the other boys and girls laughed and talked before the Bible class began. Everyone was excited about the picnic after church services.

When the class was over, Miss Emily called to Claire and Bill as they left the room. "Wait, children! I have a secret that will cheer you up. I am so excited about two people who are coming to our picnic. Can you guess who is coming from Coal Valley?"

Bill and Claire wondered who she was talking about.

Miss Emily saw their bewildered looks. "All right.
I won't make you guess," she said. "I will *tell* you
who is coming. Two of your best friends will be here.
They are the ones who taught all of us to ask, *What
would Jesus do?* I was so surprised when I discovered
that they live in the old mining town."

Claire gasped and clapped her hands over her mouth.

Bill stared wide-eyed at Miss Emily. "Oh, no!" he cried. "Not Jack and Mr. Martin!"

Miss Emily's smile faded. "I thought that would make you happy," she said, looking puzzled.

"We've got to warn them!" Bill yelled to Claire. The two of them took off running faster than they ever had run in their lives.

What Would Jesus Do?

Has someone ever made you afraid to tell the truth? Is there a time when you told the truth, even though it was hard to do?

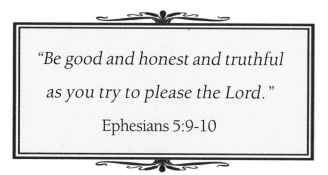

*"Be good and honest and truthful as you try to please the Lord."*

Ephesians 5:9-10

# FACING THE FIRE!

## Chapter Twenty

Racing ahead of Bill, Claire ran along the line of people coming from Coal Valley to the church. Finally she spotted Mr. Martin and Jack at the end of the line.

"Claire! Bill! What's wrong?" asked Jack as the children dashed up to him.

"Three boys are going to start a fire in Coal Valley while everyone is at the picnic!" said Claire. "They threatened to throw us down the old mine shaft if we told anyone!"

Jack looked back down the road. "Oh, no!" he shouted. "I see smoke rising above our town!"

Mr. Martin quickly gave orders. "Jack, run to the church. Tell everyone about the fire. Bill and Claire, come with me! I must go to Coal Valley. You have to be my eyes."

Jack ran up the hill while the others turned back on the road. As they hurried toward the town, Mr. Martin asked Bill, "Did you tell the boys that setting fires is wrong?"

"I should have, Mr. Martin," said Bill sadly. "But I was afraid and I ran away."

"Why didn't you come and talk to me?"

"I was too scared," Bill answered. "I ran all the way home instead of trying to find you."

"Claire," asked Mr. Martin, "couldn't you tell your father?"

Claire hung her head. "I was afraid to say anything, so I ran into the house."

Rounding the bend in the road, Mr. Martin asked, "What do you see now?"

"The smoke and flames reach so high," Bill said sadly. "Oh! Your house must be burning, too!"

Mr. Martin stood still. "I smell the smoke and feel the heat of the flames. But now I hear the sound of crying. Is that you, children?" he asked. They only sobbed.

"Bill and Claire," he said gently. "How many times did each of you run away this week?"

"I ran from the mean boys," answered Claire. "And I kept running instead of waiting for you at the road. Then I ran away instead of telling my father."

"I ran away three times, too," Bill said quietly. "This reminds me of Peter in the Bible," said Mr. Martin. "Peter turned away from Jesus three times. Then he cried. He was sorry for what he had done. Do you know what Jesus did to Peter?"

"What?" asked Bill.

Claire wiped her tears. "Jesus forgave him," she said softly.

"Yes," said Mr. Martin, putting his arm around their shoulders. "I know you are sorry for what you've done. And I know Jesus will forgive you."

Mr. Martin reached out his arms and embraced them as they clung to him. "I forgive you, too," he said tenderly. "That's what Jesus would do."

What Would Jesus Do?

Did you ever feel that you did something too bad for Jesus to forgive?

Take time right now to ask his forgiveness.

*"If we confess our sins to God, he can always be trusted to forgive us."*

1 John 1:9

To learn more about the times Peter denied Jesus, read Matthew 26:31-35, 69-75.

# FIGHTING THE FIRE!

## Chapter Twenty-One

Just as Claire arrived in Coal Valley with Mr. Martin and Bill, she saw Jack come running down the hill with more people than she could count. Everyone at the picnic had answered the call for help.

Men hollered orders and began a bucket relay from the well to the burning houses. Some people helped carry furniture from homes where fires were spreading. Several teenagers tried to beat out smaller grass fires.

Parson Henry called all the children together.
"Stay away from the burning buildings! Be sure to put
out any sparks that land in the field. You can take off
your jackets and pound the flames or stomp on the
sparks. But be careful! And help each other!"

Later, when Parson Henry stood up in front of the people, Claire hardly recognized him. His face was covered with soot. She couldn't tell which people were from Pine Ridge and which were from Coal Valley because of the blackened faces and clothes.

Then he spoke to them. "Some of us here have been learning this week what it means to follow Jesus. We're trying to always ask, *What would Jesus do?*"

Looking over the ruins of the old town, Parson Henry paused. "Ashes lie all around us," he said sadly. "Our new friends here have lost even the little they had. So I ask all of you members of Valley Church, *What would Jesus do?*"

Claire recognized the voice of a man from Pine Ridge who said, "Jesus would help build better houses than before! I'll help build."

A cheer rose from the crowd, along with choruses of, "We'll help, too!"

"Jesus would share what he had with people who lost their homes," said another man.

"We'll share our home with a Coal Valley family," called out one couple.

"So will we!" echoed several others.

"I don't have much to give," said a tall man, "but I can help build."

"I'll donate wood from my lumber mill," said a man standing in back of the crowd.

"Let's find out who owns this land," called out an old woman. "Maybe he will help rebuild."

The man standing beside Claire laughed and spoke up. "Mr. Whipple owns all this land. But don't count on any help from him. He is *Mr. Scrooge* himself!"

Claire noticed a tall boy walk up and put his hand on Mr. Martin's arm.

"I'm sorry," said the boy. "I never thought the fire would burn down your homes."

"Casey?" cried Bill. "Is that you?"

Claire hardly recognized the troublemaker with his blackened face. "Why has he come back?" she whispered to Bill.

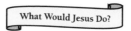

When have you worked hard to help someone else? When has someone else worked hard to help you?

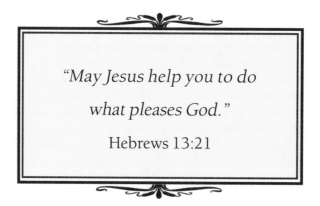

"May Jesus help you to do what pleases God."

Hebrews 13:21

# AFTER THE FIRE

## Chapter Twenty-Two

Edging closer to Bill and Mr. Martin, Claire wondered if Casey would try to hurt them. Just thinking about the day she ran away from the troublemakers made her stomach hurt.

"I was afraid of the other boys," said Casey. "So I helped start the fire. I planned to put it out later, but the flames spread too quickly." Tears streaked his face. "I was wrong. Can you ever forgive me?" he asked.

"We will forgive you," said Mr. Martin, grasping Casey's hand. "Jesus forgives each of us. And he wants us to forgive each other."

"I heard you talking to Claire and Bill about Jesus," said Casey. "Will you tell me more about Jesus?"

Mr. Martin took Casey's arm. "Of course!" he said. "Let's walk back to the church together."

Watching them walk up the road, Claire and Bill smiled. They knew that somehow Jesus would make everything all right.

During the summer, Claire and Bill joined the other church members who shared their homes, food, and building tools with Coal Valley families. Many people gave supplies, as well as their time and talents, to help rebuild the community.

One hot day, Claire and Bill walked down to Coal Valley with a group of friends. "Look around," said Claire. "So many good things have happened because people asked the four special words."

Bill nodded in agreement. "I thought the town was gone when it burned," he said. "Now people have begun to move back into their homes."

When the children arrived at the community gar-
den, an old man handed each of them a bucket. "We
need help weeding the vegetables," he said with a
smile. "Thank you for coming!"

"Will all the homes in Coal Valley be
rebuilt before winter?" Claire asked
the old man.

"All rebuilding has stopped for now," he said.
"We've run out of supplies and money. But everyone
is meeting at the church tonight. We want to pray
about what to do next."

Claire and Bill found the corn patch and began weeding. "There must be some way to raise more money for building supplies," said Bill.

"Remember when our parents organized a carnival to help buy swings for our school playground?" asked Claire. "We could put on a carnival for Coal Valley!"

Later that evening people from Pine Ridge and Coal Valley gathered for prayer and singing. Claire and Bill found Mr. Martin and shared their idea with him.

At the end of the meeting, Mr. Martin stood up. "All of us want to help rebuild. What about having a carnival and using that money to buy supplies?"

"What a great idea!" called out Parson Henry. "Let's raise money and have fun at the same time."

Other people got excited. "We'll set up booths and invite neighboring villages! Let's get started now!"

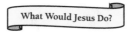
What Would Jesus Do?

Has anyone ruined something you owned?

Was it hard for you to forgive them?

Do you remember what Jesus said on the cross?

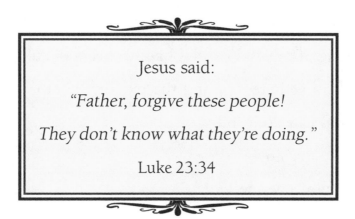

Jesus said:

*"Father, forgive these people!*

*They don't know what they're doing."*

Luke 23:34

# FALL CARNIVAL

## Chapter Twenty-Three

Claire wandered between the red and white carnival booths that had been built in the field beside Coal Valley. Gold and red autumn leaves blew across the field. The wind carried happy cheers of children who had gathered around the pitching booth.

"You can do it, Bill!"

"Hit it again!"

"You're a winner!"

Claire hurried to the front of the crowd just as Bill pitched a ball toward a row of wooden rabbits at the back of the booth.

*Wham! Whack!*

The speeding ball knocked over the rabbit.

"That's nine!" hollered Jack. "One more hit and we'll have a new county champion!"

"Hooray, Bill!" yelled Claire, jumping up and down. She knew how badly Bill wanted to win this prize. He was saving all his money to buy the Blue Blazer bicycle in the hardware store window.

Claire held her breath as Bill picked up another ball. She watched his forehead break out in a sweat. He threw the ball as hard as he could.

*Wham! Whack!*

"That's ten!" shouted Jack. Everyone cheered and slapped Bill on the back.

A tall man with a mustache rang the bell and held
up Bill's arm. "Here he is! The champion pitcher of
our county—Bill Hamilton!" the man announced
loudly. "And we have a special prize for him as the
winner of our softball pitching contest!"

Claire's heart pounded as she proudly watched the announcer drop one...two...three silver dollars into Bill's hand.

Later, when Bill was alone with Claire and Jack, he opened his hand and stared at the shiny coins.

"Wowie!" he said. "I've never *seen* a silver dollar before! Now I own three of them!" He looked up at Claire and Jack with a grin. "Just think of what this money can buy! What shall I do with it?"

The three friends looked at each other and smiled. Together they repeated the four special words they had learned to say every day: *What would Jesus do?*

What Would Jesus Do?

How do you spend your money?

Do you ask Jesus how you should spend it?

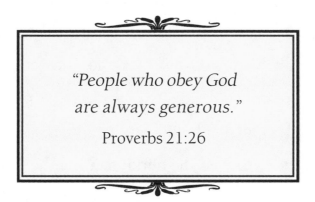

*"People who obey God
are always generous."*

Proverbs 21:26

# BIG AWARD!

## Chapter Twenty-Four

W hat would Jesus want you to do with
your prize money?" Claire asked Bill.

"I'm not sure," said Bill. "Let's go find Mr. Martin."
Searching through the crowd, they found Mr. Martin
sitting at the pie booth. Bill handed him the silver
dollars, then watched the blind man feel the coins
with his fingers.

"I would like a Blue Blazer Bike," Bill told Mr. Martin. "But maybe that is selfish. This money could help people build new homes. Do you think Jesus would spend money on himself? Would he save it?"

Mr. Martin smiled. "Don't you think Jesus might do all three? You could give a dollar to God's work in Coal Valley and you could save a dollar. Then you would have one dollar left to spend on something you'd like."

"Oh, yes!" said Bill. "I like that idea."

*Ding! Dong! Ding!* A loud bell sounded from the carnival stage.

A man in a blue uniform stood beside the large ribbon-covered box and announced, "It is time for our exciting Carnival Grand Prize! The L & R Railroad is giving away four tickets on Monday's express train. Our winner plus three friends will receive a free trip to Springdale, the capital of our great state!"

Reaching into the box, the man pulled out a card and announced: "The winner of this train ride is... Jack Browning!"

Claire gasped. Jack just stood with his mouth wide open.

"Jack Browning!" called the man on the stage. "Come and get your four tickets!"

"Jack! They called your name!" said Claire, pulling on his sleeve.

"But, but...I *can't* go to Springdale!" said Jack. "I don't have money to pay for meals or a place to sleep!" He kept protesting while Bill and Claire pushed him to the platform to receive his tickets.

Later, when they walked home, Jack held up the tickets. "What do you think Jesus wants me to do with these?"

"I don't know," said Bill. He held up one shiny dollar. "But I think Jesus wants *me* to give this to you for your trip."

"*I* think Jesus wants *me* to find a place for you to stay," said Claire. "My cousin Amy lives in Springdale."

"Then I will go!" said Jack. "But I am not going to take your money, Bill. And I won't stay with your cousin, Claire—unless you both come with me! I won't go to Springdale without my two best friends and Mr. Martin!"

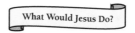

What Would Jesus Do?

What do you have that you can share?

How can you share and cooperate with others today?

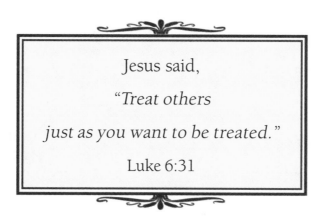

Jesus said,

"*Treat others*

*just as you want to be treated.*"

Luke 6:31

Read how the first Christians shared in Acts 4:32-37.

# TRAIN TRIP

## Chapter Twenty-Five

On Monday, friends and relatives walked with Claire and Bill to the train station where Jack and Mr. Martin were waiting.

Bill reached into his pocket and handed two silver dollars to his mother. "Be sure and give one of these to buy supplies for Coal Valley. And put one in the bank to save. We're taking the other dollar to Springdale."

*Tooooooot! Tooooooot!* The steam engine pulled into the train station. Claire hugged her father good-bye and climbed aboard with Bill, Jack, and Mr. Martin. They found their seats and waved out the window as the train left the station.

Jack frowned as he watched the countryside speed by. "Do trains ever have bad wrecks?" he asked.

"Yes," said Claire. "But don't be afraid. Remember the song we learned at church." She started singing and the boys quickly joined in.

> *He's got the whole world in his hands,*
>
> *He's got the whole wide world in his hands,*
>
> *He's got the L & R Railroad in his hands,*
>
> *He's got the whole world in his hands!*

Mr. Martin said, "God has everything in his hands, even this railroad. Always remember God's promise— *everything* will work for our good when we love Jesus."

An hour later, the train arrived at Springdale.

"Wow!" said Bill. "What a big city."

Jack told Mr. Martin, "I see lots of buildings. The streets are full of wagons and carriages."

"There are many people," said Claire. "And they're all dressed up. Are city people different from us?"

"No, they are just like us," Mr. Martin answered. "But many of them don't know how much Jesus loves them and they don't know how to follow him." Before stepping off the train, the blind man pulled the three children close.

"God sent me here to pray for the people of this city," Mr. Martin said quietly. "While you visit Amy, I'll be walking the streets of this city and praying. God sent you here for a reason, too. Before you leave town, you will find out what that reason is."

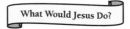
What Would Jesus Do?

Think about the neighborhood and city where you live. Who can you pray for?

*"Stay alert and keep praying for God's people."*
Ephesians 6:18b

# TICKET TROUBLE

## Chapter Twenty-Six

Outside the train station, Mr. Martin found a carriage that would take the children to Amy's house. After paying the driver, Mr. Martin hugged each child. "I will see you Saturday morning. Be sure to have Amy's parents bring you back here by ten o'clock," he reminded Claire. "I'll be praying for your visit."

The children stood by the carriage and watched him walk toward Main Street. Then Claire reached into her pocket. Her face grew pale and she quickly tugged at Jack's sleeve. "Jack!" she said. "I can't find my ticket for the trip back home! Did I give it to you?"

Jack frowned at her. "I don't remember."

"Please check them," Claire said. "Make sure you have all four of our tickets."

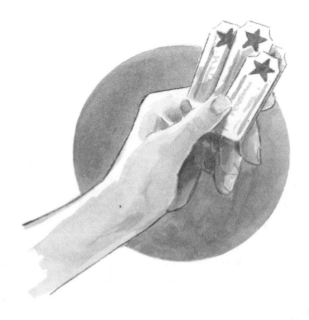

Jack pulled the tickets out of his pocket and began to count them. One, two, three, four. Suddenly, Claire saw a hand from the crowd reach out and snatch them away from Jack.

"Help!" yelled Jack.

"Stop that boy!" cried Claire. "He stole our tickets!" She pointed to a tall boy in overalls who quickly vanished into the crowd.

"Hurry up and climb in," scolded the driver of the carriage. He flicked the reins impatiently. "Come on! We're leaving," he warned.

The children quickly climbed into the carriage. Tears ran down Claire's cheeks as she watched the boys' frightened faces. They huddled together as the carriage bumped along the cobblestone streets.

"I'm so sorry, Jack," said Claire. "This is all my fault. I should have remembered that I gave you my return ticket stub. We would still have the tickets if I had not asked you to check them."

"How will we ever get back home?" asked Bill.

Claire closed her eyes. "I don't know," she said quietly, "but let's ask Jesus."

What Would Jesus Do?

What do you do when things go wrong? Will you trust Jesus to help you?

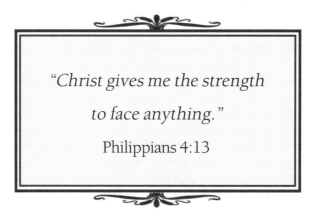

*"Christ gives me the strength*

*to face anything."*

Philippians 4:13

To learn about a man who had faith even when his little girl died, read Matthew 9:18-26.

# COUSIN AMY

## Chapter Twenty-Seven

By the time the carriage driver stopped on State Street, the three children felt sure Jesus would take care of them.

When the driver opened the coach door, the children stared at the beautiful mansion in front of them. "Here's the house," he said. "Now hurry and climb out!" The children scrambled down the coach steps.

The carriage drove away and Claire's cousin, Amy Starr, came running out the mansion's front door. "I'm so glad you came to visit us!" said Amy. She led them to a box in her back yard. "Come and see my new pet," she said. Claire heard a squeaky yelp as Amy reached under a blanket and lifted up a scrawny puppy.

"Look at my sweet puppy!" said Amy. "We found her here on our porch last week. I named her Bitsy."

"Amy!" called a girl from the house next door. "Is that your cousin and her friends from Pine Ridge?"

"Yes, Penny! Come over and meet them," said Amy. Penny glanced back toward her house before she ran across the lawn toward Amy's porch.

"This is my friend, Penny Whipple," Amy said to the children as Penny approached.

Bang! Back at Penny's house a door slammed. A stocky man, dressed in a brown suit, stepped out onto the porch. He scowled and twirled his mustache. "Penelope!" he snapped in a gruff voice. "I don't want you to play with that scruffy dog or those straggly children. Amy Starr and her family are not *our* kind of people anymore."

"Come back home, right now!" he called loudly.

"I'm sorry," Penny whispered sadly to the children. She turned and walked slowly back home. Without a word, Amy dashed inside her house, tears streaming down her cheeks.

"What's wrong?" Bill asked Claire.

"I don't know," said Claire. "But we'd better follow Amy."

Inside the house, they saw Mrs. Starr lying down with her leg bandaged. Claire and the boys stood quietly by the door as Amy cried in her mother's arms.

"I didn't know how to tell you, dear," Amy's mother said to her. "Your father has lost his job. Mr. Whipple is angry because we can't pay our bills. He has sent your father to jail until the money we owe him is paid back. Now we must pack all our belongings. We need to move at once to a smaller and cheaper place."

Claire and the boys looked wide-eyed at each other, wondering what they would do next. Claire quickly grabbed the boys' hands. "Dear Jesus," she prayed softly. "Help Amy's mother find a place to live. And show us what you want us to do."

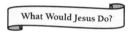

What Would Jesus Do?

When has someone been mean or unfair to you? What did you do? Does it still make you feel sad?

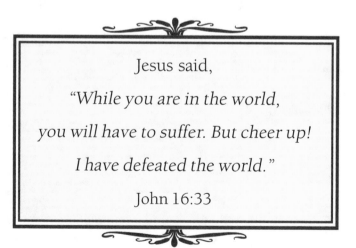

Jesus said,

*"While you are in the world,*

*you will have to suffer. But cheer up!*

*I have defeated the world."*

John 16:33

# MOVING TROUBLES

## Chapter Twenty-Eight

During the next few days, Claire and the boys packed boxes of clothes, dishes, pots, and pans. Friends of Amy's mother found them a run-down apartment in a section of town called Southside. Other neighbors helped them move all the boxes.

"Thank you, Claire," said Amy's mother as she rested in bed after the move. "You and your friends helped pack and move everything! Jesus sent you here at just the right time."

Claire handed her aunt a glass of water. "How will you pay your bills when you can't work, Aunt Ruth?"

"I've been thinking about that," said Amy's mother. "I have to stay off my leg for a while, but I can still crochet. Maybe there is a way to sell my hankies and tablecloths."

Bill reached into his pocket. "I have a silver dollar, Mrs. Starr," he said. "And I know what Jesus would do with it. He would buy some extra groceries for you."

"I'll go to the store with you," offered Claire.

"Me, too," said Jack.

"I think I should stay with Mother," said Amy.

Claire, Bill, and Jack walked down the apartment stairs and into the crowded streets.

Claire looked up and down the street as they walked. "Southside is not a nice place to live," she said. "I'm glad I'm not trying to find a grocery store by myself. I get so mixed up in my directions. I have no idea how to get back to Amy's house."

Bill held up his shiny coin. "I didn't know my silver dollar would help feed a family in trouble," he said with a smile. "Maybe that's the reason why God sent me to this town."

Suddenly two arms shoved Bill into the street. The silver dollar flew out of his hand. A barefoot boy grabbed the coin and ran down the street.

"Stop that thief!" yelled Bill.

"Help!" screamed Claire and Jack.

Everyone in the noisy crowd ignored the children. The three of them ran down the street chasing after the boy, who quickly outran them.

Bill sat down on the curb, tears streaming down his cheeks. "I'm hungry! Now we have no food and no money. What are we going to do? And how will we ever get back home?"

"Jesus will help us," said Claire. She and Jack sat down beside Bill to rest their tired feet. "Dear Jesus," they prayed quietly. "You know our problem. Help us not to worry. Let us know what you want us to do."

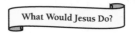

What Would Jesus Do?

What do you worry about?

What would you tell someone who is worried?

*"God cares for you,*
*so turn all your worries over to him."*

1 Peter 5:7

When King Herod planned to kill Peter, many people prayed. Read Acts 12:5-17 to find out what God did.

# A BIG MISTAKE!

## Chapter Twenty-Nine

Resting her elbows on her knees, Claire sat and watched people bustle up and down the busy street. No one paid any attention to the three children sitting on the curb.

"I don't know what we can do without any money," said Claire. "And I don't know how we will ever get back home, but I'm going to keep on praying."

"Hey, be careful! Watch out!" hollered two men standing by the children. Suddenly the crowd on the street jumped aside as a carriage charged around the corner. It narrowly missed hitting Claire and the boys.

"Get out of my way!" yelled the driver at the children as he pulled the horses to a stop. The fancy carriage looked out of place among the ragged crowds and run-down buildings.

A grumpy-looking man pushed open the door and stepped down from the coach.

Claire gasped. "Oh, no! It's Mr. Whipple!"

The man marched up to the hardware store, opened the door, and called out, "Mike Mallory, hand over your rent money NOW, or you'll be sent to jail!"

"Look!" Bill whispered, pointing at the carriage.

Claire saw a barefoot boy with a pocket knife run up to the coach. He cut the leather harness and started to run off with the horse. Bill and Jack rushed over and stopped him. They grabbed the reins from the boy, who quickly ran away.

"Horse thieves!" shouted Mr. Whipple. He stomped over to the carriage and grabbed Bill and Jack by their shirts. "This is my valuable horse!" he said, handing the boys over to his driver. "Take these robbers to jail!"

"But sir, you're mistaken!" said Bill. "We didn't try to steal your horse."

"You heard Mr. Whipple," said the coachman. He finished hitching the horse to the carriage and grabbed their arms. "Start walking, you rascals. You're headed for jail."

Bill prayed out loud, "Jesus, help us!"

"Be quiet! And keep moving!" the driver ordered as he hurried them down the street.

Claire's heart pounded with fear, but she couldn't say a word. The lump in her throat felt as big as the carriage. Her eyes grew blurry with tears while she watched her friends walk out of sight.

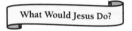

When have you felt upset lately?

Were you ever blamed for something you didn't do?

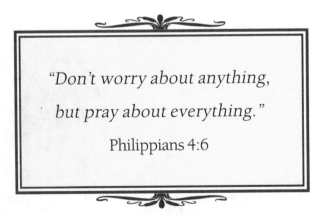

"Don't worry about anything,

but pray about everything."

Philippians 4:6

# LOST AND ALONE

## Chapter Thirty

With Bill and Jack gone, Claire sat down on the curb. She felt lost and alone and more frightened than ever. What would happen to the boys? How would she get back to Amy's apartment?

"Dear Jesus, please help Bill and Jack," she prayed. "And show me where to go." She couldn't stop crying as she stumbled down the street.

Claire nearly tripped over the bare feet of a child sitting by the alley garbage can. He looked so sad that she almost forgot her own troubles. "Oh Jesus," she prayed. "Help that little boy. He looks unhappy. Let him know that you love him."

Farther down the street, Claire passed an elderly woman selling flowers. "Please buy some mums," said the old woman, holding out a bouquet in her gnarled fingers.

"I'm sorry," said Claire. "I don't have any money."
Walking past the woman, Claire prayed quietly, "Dear
Jesus, bless her and take care of her."

Claire's eyes brightened. "Now I understand," she
said to herself. "This is what Mr. Martin is doing. And
this is what Jesus would do if he were here. I will
pray for these people, too." Claire felt calmer now as
she prayed. There were so many who needed her prayers.

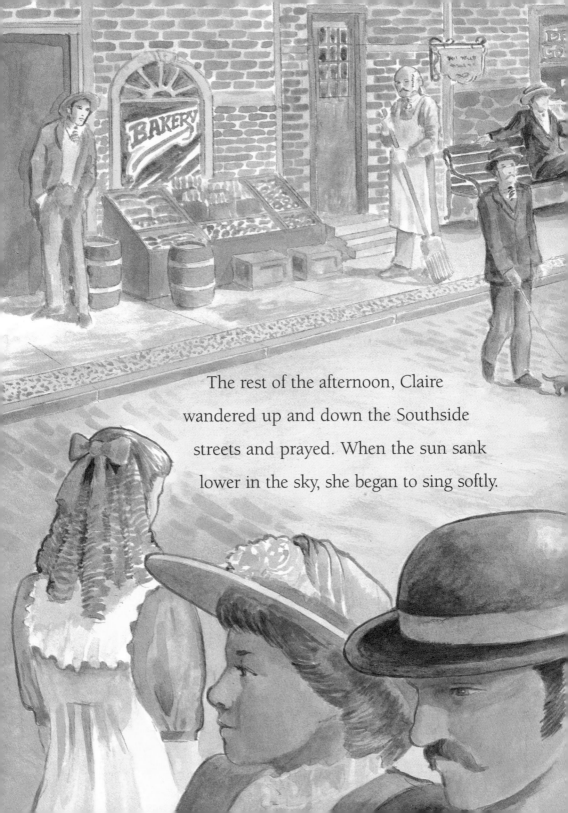

The rest of the afternoon, Claire
wandered up and down the Southside
streets and prayed. When the sun sank
lower in the sky, she began to sing softly.

*He's got the great big city in his hands,*

*He's got my friends and family in his hands,*

*He's got everybody here in his hands,*

*He's got the whole world in—*

Suddenly Claire heard a squeaky bark. Through the crowd, she spotted a black and white dog. "Bitsy!" called Claire. The dog looked around. It *was* Bitsy! And Amy was with her!

Claire ran to her cousin. "I was so lost and scared by myself," she said as they hugged each other.

"We were worried when you didn't come back," said Amy. "Where are the boys?"

Tears filled Claire's eyes again. "They are in jail! Mr. Whipple thought they were stealing his horse."

"Oh, no!" cried Amy. "What will we do now?"

"I don't know, but Jesus does," said Claire. "He will show us. But first I want to thank him for helping me find *you*."

As Claire closed her eyes to pray, she heard foot-
steps. She looked up to see a young man carrying a
big tray of carved figures.

Who are the people that you see every day?
What could you pray about for each of them?

"Never stop praying,

especially for others."

Ephesians 6:18a

Read what Jesus said about prayer in Matthew 6:5-13.

# ANOTHER NEW FRIEND
## Chapter Thirty-One

Claire watched the young man walk up to her cousin. He carefully held a tray filled with wooden carvings. "Hi, Amy," he said with a smile. "Who's your friend?"

"Hello, David. This is my cousin Claire," said Amy. "And Claire, this is David Christopher. He is one of our new Southside neighbors."

"David's father is out of town looking for work," explained Amy. "He taught David how to carve. David sells his carvings here at the market. That's how I found out where to sell Mother's crocheting."

"What have you sold this afternoon?" David asked.

"Five hankies," said Amy. "Mother will be happy to have fifty cents! Have you sold anything?"

David smiled. "It was my best day yet. I made ninety-five cents!" He held up the tray so Claire could see the carved dollhouse furniture, tops, crosses, and praying hands.

"I brought Amy here and I promised to meet her at the end of the day to walk her home," said David, glancing down the alley. "These streets are dangerous. Thieves even rob people during the day."

"Bill's silver dollar was stolen today," said Claire.

David frowned. "I'm sorry about that. Southside bullies are a big problem. I never know if I will make it home safely. I wish we could do something about it."

"We can do something!" Claire said cheerfully. "My friends and I always ask four special words."

"What words?" asked David.

"We say: *What Would Jesus Do?*" Claire explained. "And then we ask Jesus to show us what to do."

"I like that idea," said David. While he walked, he began praying with his eyes open. "Jesus, what would you do for all of these people? How can I help?"

"Look!" said Claire, pointing across the street. "If we had a building like that empty warehouse, we could invite people to come and hear about Jesus."

Just then Bitsy barked at a kitten peeking around the alley.

"Look, Amy! A kitten!" said Claire. "Maybe we should take it home." Claire and Amy headed into the alley. "We'll be right back, David," said Claire.

What Would Jesus Do?

Take time to pray for those who live around you. Ask Jesus what you could do for them.

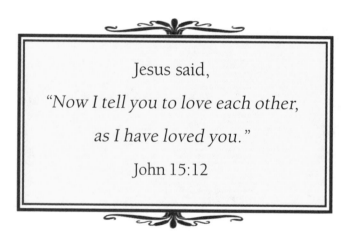

Jesus said,

*"Now I tell you to love each other,*

*as I have loved you."*

John 15:12

# BIG BULLIES

## Chapter Thirty-Two

"Here kitty, kitty," called Claire as she followed the kitten into the dark alley. Suddenly, someone grabbed her arm. "Amy!" shrieked Claire. "Go back! Get help!"

"David! Help!" screamed Amy in the darkness. But it was too late. She was also caught. And when David came rushing into the alley, the group of barefoot bullies grabbed him, too.

"Let the girls go!" yelled David.

"Keep quiet!" ordered the biggest bully. "We've been watching you kids. You made good money today. Now hand it over." He held out a burlap bag. Amy and David dropped their coins into it.

He stuck the bag in front of Claire. "Give us your money, too!" he said. Claire held back her tears as she shook her head. "I don't have any money. But you need something better than money. You need Jesus! I'm praying for you and so is our friend, Mr. Martin."

The big bully drew closer. "Mr. Martin?" he asked. "Hey! Are you talking about an old blind man?"

Claire recognized the bully. He was the thief who had stolen Bill's dollar and the train tickets! She spoke up boldly. "Yes! Blind Mr. Martin is walking the streets of this city right now, praying for people like you."

The gang leader looked closely at her. "I met Mr. Martin two years ago," he said. "I prayed with him and asked Jesus to be my Savior. But instead of following Jesus, I went my own way."

David stepped up. "What's your name?" he asked.

"I'm Joe," said the boy.

"God loves you, Joe," said David. "And God has a great plan for your life. Stop stealing and come back to Jesus." David turned to the other boys. "We want to share Jesus with all of you. Come to our meeting tomorrow night at the warehouse across the street."

Claire wondered what David was talking about.

"Joe," asked David. "Will you help tell others about our meeting?"

The other bullies sneered. "Who wants to come to a stupid meeting?" they said. "If we come, we'll make trouble!" Then they turned and ran down the alley.

After the other bullies left, Joe said quietly, "I *will* come tomorrow night, but not to make trouble. I want my life to be different." Before he left, he dropped the money bag by Claire's feet.

When have you been a good example for others? Name some people you know who have done good and brave things.

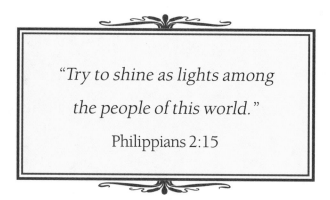

*"Try to shine as lights among the people of this world."*

Philippians 2:15

## IN JAIL

### Chapter Thirty-Three

That night, Bill and Jack sat together on the bare floor of a cold jailhouse cell.

"Was Jesus ever in jail?" asked Jack.

"I don't think so," said Bill. "But Paul, one of Jesus' followers, was put in jail a lot. Once Paul and his friend, Silas, were whipped and then locked up in jail."

"I wonder if they felt as scared as I feel," said Jack.
"What did they do?"

"Instead of complaining and thinking about their
troubles, they thought about God," said Bill. "They
sang and praised God all night. And God sent an
earthquake to set them free!"

Bill began quietly singing, "I have decided to follow Jesus." Gradually his voice gained strength. "I HAVE decided to follow Jesus."

Jack joined in and they sang out boldly, "We have decided to follow Jesus. We have decided to—"

"Stop that racket!" hollered voices down the hall.

The man in the next cell hollered back. "Leave the boys alone!" he said as he looked into the boys' cell. "Keep singing, boys. That song gives me strength."

Soon other voices joined the boys as they sang. After a while, the whole jailhouse shook with their singing. When the songs ended, the man asked Bill and Jack, "Why are you boys in here?"

Bill and Jack explained what had happened to them. And they were surprised to discover that the man in the next cell was Amy's father!

"Most of us in this jail owe money to Mr. Whipple," said Mr. Starr. "He is a mean and selfish man."

"Jesus prayed for the men who nailed him to the cross," said Bill. "Let's pray together for Mr. Whipple."

"Yes," agreed Mr. Starr. "Only God can change that man's heart." Together in the darkness, he and the boys prayed for the man who had put them in jail.

When they finally lay down to sleep, Bill whispered to Jack, "Mr. Martin is praying as he walks the streets of this city. Maybe God sent us to jail to pray for these people."

Jack whispered back, "Do you think God will keep us in jail so we can tell other prisoners about Jesus?"

"I hope not," said Bill with a shiver. "But I am willing to do what Jesus wants, even if it means staying here a long time."

What Would Jesus Do?

Who has treated you unfairly?
Ask Jesus to help you forgive and pray for them.

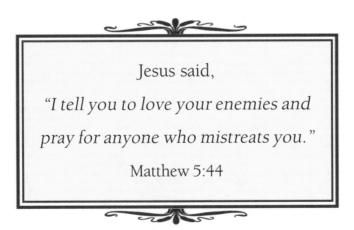

Jesus said,
*"I tell you to love your enemies and pray for anyone who mistreats you."*
Matthew 5:44

# BIG PLANS

## Chapter Thirty-Four

That night when David took the girls back home, Amy invited him to share their left-over biscuits and turnip stew. Claire poured a small bowl of milk for the stray kitten and fed biscuit crumbs to Bitsy.

After dinner, the children washed dishes while Amy's mother crocheted more fancy hankies and tablecloths to sell.

"David," said Claire. "Why did you invite those bullies to a meeting tomorrow in the warehouse?"

David grinned at her. "Well, you told me to ask the question, *What would Jesus do?* And I thought Jesus would want us to tell people around here how much he loves them."

"Yes," agreed Amy. She paused and wiped another dish. "But there is one problem. How can we have a meeting when we don't have a place to meet?"

"I know that God can do the impossible," said Claire. "Maybe the owner of the warehouse would let us use it." Her face lit up at the thought. "We could call it the *Sharehouse* because we'll share the good news about Jesus. And perhaps we could share a meal with everyone, too."

"Where would you get the food?" asked Amy. "Who would cook it?"

Claire thought for a minute. "I don't know," she said. "But I believe that's what Jesus would do."

"You will need a sign to invite people to your meeting," said Amy's mother. "Let's make a banner from this large piece of cloth. I will sew a cross on it."

"I'll paint the four special words on the cloth," said Claire. She looked around at everyone. "We can pray and work together, but only God can make this meeting happen. Let's trust God for a miracle."

After they joined hands and prayed together, David picked up his tray of wooden figures. "I will find out who owns the warehouse," he said, "and come back here tomorrow morning."

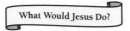

What Would Jesus Do?

Is there something that seems impossible to you? Are you trusting God for a miracle?

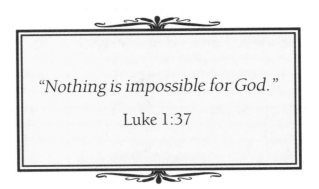

*"Nothing is impossible for God."*

Luke 1:37

To find out what happened when God's people faced an impossible battle, read 2 Chronicles 20:1-30.

# MEETING THE OWNER
## Chapter Thirty-Five

Early the next morning, David arrived at Amy's home. From the smile on his face, Claire knew he had good news.

"I found out who owns the warehouse," David told the girls. "And I know where he lives on the other side of town. It is a long walk. We will need to get started soon."

The three children walked along, enjoying the
warm sunny morning. Claire laughed
as she kicked the mounds of golden
leaves lying on the streets.
"I like October," she said.

"I like this part of town," said Amy. "It reminds me of where I used to live." As they walked further, Claire noticed that Amy looked around anxiously.

"Where are we going, David?" asked Amy. "These trees and the park look just like my old neighborhood. Oh! There is my old house!" said Amy. "On that next street corner!"

"Amy, what a surprise! You lived right next door to the man who owns the empty warehouse," said David.

Amy stopped and stared across the street. "No!" she cried. "We should never have come here!"

Then Claire also recognized Mr. Whipple's house, and she remembered how he had yelled at his daughter, Penny. Claire groaned. "It *will* take a miracle to use the warehouse. Mr. Whipple owns that mansion. And he is the meanest man I have ever met!"

The children's hopes faded as they slowly walked up the front steps to the house. David knocked at the door, while the girls waited nervously.

Penny opened the front door. "What are all of you doing here?" she asked.

"We've come to talk to your father," said Amy.

"Oh, Father is very upset!" said Penny. "He had a terrible dream last night. That is all he talks about. Now he says he's waiting for an angel. Please come in."

The children stepped into the house. Claire saw Mr. Whipple sitting in his chair, still wearing his robe and nightcap. His breakfast lay untouched on the table beside him. When Mr. Whipple looked up and saw the three children, he leaned forward.

"Aren't you Amy Starr, the girl who used to live next door? Please don't be afraid. I'm so sorry for the way I treated your family and your friends."

Amy and Claire stepped closer to Mr. Whipple. Claire looked into his eyes, then spoke boldly. "If you please, sir, we've come to ask you to do something."

Mr. Whipple's face burst into a smile. "All morning I've been begging God to send someone to tell me what to do next. You are an answer to my prayer!"

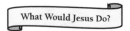

What Would Jesus Do?

Do you know someone who is mean and selfish? Are you willing to pray for them and talk to them about Jesus?

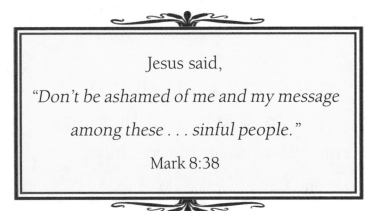

Jesus said,

"Don't be ashamed of me and my message among these . . . sinful people."

Mark 8:38

# A NEW MAN

## Chapter Thirty-Six

Mr. Whipple invited the children to sit down on his big sofa. When he shared what had happened to him, Claire could hardly believe her ears.

"Last night I had a frightening dream," he told the children. "I saw Judgment Day. And I saw the finger of God pointing at me! Then God spoke to me."

"God said, 'I see your heart. I know what you are like. The only thing you care about is yourself. You throw innocent men and boys in prison. You don't care about the people who live in your run-down houses. What about the taverns you own, where men and women waste their time and money drinking and gambling? And what have you ever done to help others?"

Mr. Whipple continued, "Suddenly I saw myself as a proud and greedy man who doesn't love anyone—not even God! I felt so ashamed. I got down on my knees and cried." Tears trickled down his cheeks.

"Don't despair, Mr. Whipple," said Claire. "Ask God to forgive you."

"But I hurt Amy's family and many other people," said Mr. Whipple. "How can I ever make up for it?"

"Nobody can *make up* for the wrongs they've done," said David. "That's why all of us need a Savior."

"That's why God sent Jesus," Claire said quietly. "Jesus died on the cross, for me *and* for you. Now he wants us to love other people the same way he loves us."

"Oh," sighed Mr. Whipple. "Now I understand." He knelt by a chair and bowed his head.

The three children knelt beside him. Even Penny knelt as her father asked Jesus to forgive him and to change his heart.

When he finished praying, Mr. Whipple turned his face toward Claire, Amy, and David. "God sent you to tell me about Jesus. Thank you so much for coming here today!"

Claire smiled. "We came here to ask if we could use your warehouse for a meeting tonight. We want to share Jesus with the Southside people. Many of them are hungry and we want to feed them." She felt bolder as she looked into his changed eyes. "Could you please help us? We don't have any money."

"Of course I will help you! Use my warehouse! My driver will take you there now," said Mr. Whipple.

"Get everything ready for your meeting and I will come soon," said Mr. Whipple. "There is something important Jesus wants me to do *first*."

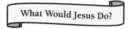

Have you given your life to Jesus?

What would you want Jesus to change in your heart or your attitude?

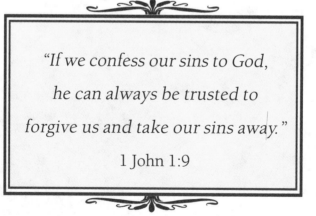

*"If we confess our sins to God,*
*he can always be trusted to*
*forgive us and take our sins away."*
1 John 1:9

# SHAREHOUSE MEETING
## Chapter Thirty-Seven

C laire, Amy, and David climbed into Mr. Whipple's carriage and sang all the way to the warehouse. As soon as they got to the warehouse, they hung up the banner and arranged chairs and benches for the meeting.

Claire felt worried. "Do you think Joe has spread the word about our meeting?" she asked David. "Will people see our banner? Will anybody come tonight?"

Suddenly the warehouse doors swung open. In walked Mr. Whipple, followed by a large group of men and boys.

"Daddy!" cried Amy, running to greet a tall man. When Claire saw Bill and Jack, she ran to meet them.

Mr. Whipple climbed up on a chair. "ATTENTION, please!" he said. "I want all of you men and boys to know why I set you free."

"Jesus has changed my life! I'm sorry I sent you to jail. Please forgive me." Reaching into his pocket, Mr. Whipple took out his billfold. "I will repay each of you for the work you missed. And I also want to invite you to work for me in Coal Valley. Bill and Jack told me about the fire that burned many homes. I will pay you all good wages."

The warehouse doors swung open again. Claire watched more people arrive at the warehouse. "Joe must have done a good job spreading the word!" she said to David. "Look how many people have come!"

Then cooks and waiters, sent by Mr. Whipple, carried in steaming pots of potatoes, platters of baked fish, and bowls of fruit. They set out the feast and began to serve everyone.

An old woman was the first one in line. She smiled broadly as she walked past Claire with her plateful of food. "It's the best meal I've ever had, dearie!" she said to Claire. Then Claire recognized her as the flower seller she had prayed for yesterday.

The boys and Claire stood side by side, watching more and more people stream into the warehouse.

"I can hardly believe how many people are here," said Bill. "Your plan really worked, Claire! I can't wait to hear what you are going to say to everyone tonight."

What Would Jesus Do?

What are you willing to do for other people?

Is there anyone you can help feed?

With whom can you share the good news of Jesus?

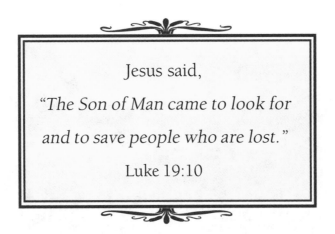

Jesus said,

*"The Son of Man came to look for and to save people who are lost."*

Luke 19:10

# CHANGED HEARTS!

## Chapter Thirty-Eight

After everyone had eaten their fill of the delicious supper, Claire and David stood up in front of the warehouse. David held up one of his carved wooden crosses and said, "We invited you here tonight because God wants to give you the most important gift you could ever receive—the gift of Jesus, God's own Son."

"Jesus loves each one of you," said David. "He wants to be your Savior and your Friend."

Claire pointed to the banner. "We have asked Jesus to be our Savior. And we are learning to ask four special words every day," she said. "Those words are: *What Would Jesus Do?* Then we try to live like Jesus would. All of you can do this, too!"

Many people received Jesus as their Savior that night. They ended the meeting with singing:

*We have decided to follow Jesus;*

*We have decided to follow Jesus;*

*We have decided to follow Jesus;*

*In every way; through every day.*

As the last people left the warehouse, Claire spotted Mr. Martin. "I didn't know *you* were here!" she said, giving him a hug.

"Joe found me and brought me," said Mr. Martin.

Joe's face shone with joy as he stood beside Mr. Martin. "I thought I wasn't good enough to follow Jesus because I had done too many bad things," said Joe. "But Mr. Martin told me that Jesus loves me and has already paid for the wrong I've done. Now I want to follow Jesus. And I want to do what he would do."

Joe reached out and put something in Claire's hand. "Will you please forgive me for making trouble for you and your friends?"

Claire looked in her hand. There lay Bill's not-so-shiny silver dollar and the four train tickets! "I never thought I would see these again," said Claire. "Yes, I'll forgive you. That's what Jesus would do."

The next morning, Claire boarded the train with the boys and Mr. Martin. She noticed Mr. Whipple and a group of workers climb aboard, too.

"There are many reasons why God sent us to Springdale," Claire said to Bill and Jack. "Look at Mr. Whipple. Many lives are changed. Now more people are doing what Jesus would do!"

Bill nodded. "Yes. Hundreds of people all over Pine Ridge, Coal Valley, and Springdale have begun to ask, *What would Jesus do?*"

"Perhaps someday there will be *thousands*," said Claire. "Or even *millions!*"

Bill smiled broadly. "Maybe people all around the whole world will ask this question!" he said.

Claire's eyes sparkled. "Especially if we just keep asking what Jesus would do—and then do it!"

What Would Jesus Do?

Will you be one of those who ask, *What would Jesus do?*

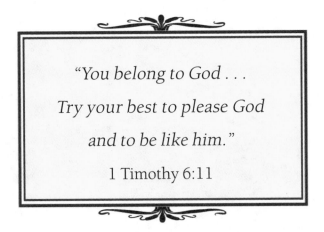
*"You belong to God . . .*
*Try your best to please God*
*and to be like him."*
1 Timothy 6:11